KEVIN DURANT

Champion Basketball Star

Ryan Nagelhout

Enslow Publishing
101 W. 23rd Street
Suite 240
New York, NY 10011
USA

enslow.com

Published in 2018 by Enslow Publishing, LLC.

101 W. 23rd Street, Suite 240, New York, NY 10011

Library of Congress Cataloging-in-Publication Data

Names: Nagelhout, Ryan, author.
Title: Kevin Durant : champion basketball star / Ryan Nagelhout.
Description: New York, NY : Enslow Publishing, 2018. | Series: Sports Star
  Champions | Includes bibliographical references and index. | Audience:
  Grade 6-8.
Identifiers: LCCN 2017003133| ISBN 9780766086920 (library-bound) | ISBN
  9780766087477 (pbk.) | ISBN 9780766087484 (6-pack)
Subjects: LCSH: Durant, Kevin, 1988—Juvenile literature. | Basketball
  players—United States—Biography—Juvenile literature. | African American
  basketball players—Biography—Juvenile literature.
Classification: LCC GV884.D868 N34 2018 | DDC 796.323092 [B]—dc23
LC record available at https://lccn.loc.gov/2017003133

Printed in the United States of America

To Our Readers: We have done our best to make sure all websites in this book were active and appropriate when we went to press. However, the author and the publisher have no control over and assume no liability for the material available on those websites or on any websites they may link to. Any comments or suggestions can be sent by email to customerservice@enslow.com.

Photo Credits: Cover, pp. 1, 35 Vaughn Ridley/Getty Images; pp. 4, 33 Mike Ehrmann/Getty Images; p. 8 MCT/Tribune News Media/Getty Images; pp. 11, 15 The Washington Post/Getty Images; pp. 12, 17 Robert Beck/Sports Illustrated/Getty Images; pp. 18, 23 Icon Sport Wire/Getty Images; p. 19 Jamie Squire/Getty Images; p. 25 Jonathan Ferrey/Getty Images; p. 27 Sporting News Archive/Getty Images; p. 29 John W. McDonough/Sports Illustrated/Getty Images; p. 31 Frederic J. Brown/AFP/Getty Images; p. 32 Ronald Martinez/Getty Images; p. 36 © AP Images; p. 39 Ezra Shaw/Getty Images; p. 41 Joe Scarnici/Stringer/Getty Images; p. 43 Jason Miller/Getty Images.

Contents

Kevin Durant has grown into one of the best pure scorers in the NBA and is part of the Golden State Warriors team that has dominated the NBA in recent years.

Introduction:
Defining Greatness

Kevin Durant is very familiar with the idea of being second best. In his senior year of high school, he was considered the second-best basketball prospect in the country. He was the second overall pick in the National Basketball Association (NBA) draft in 2007. He's been a runner-up in the NBA Finals and the Western Conference Finals and in voting for the league's Most Valuable Player (MVP) Award. Durant has had successes in his career and emerged as one of the NBA's best talents, but often he's thought of as a player who comes up short.

Basketball stars are often described as the next coming of a previous superstar. But Durant has often appeared to writers and analysts as one of the most difficult NBA stars to categorize.

"Kevin Durant, just barely arrived into the superstar club, is in many ways the purest example of a memory maker in the league today," wrote Bethlehem Shoals in *FreeDarko Presents the Undisputed Guide to Pro Basketball History* in 2010. Shoals—the pen name for writer Nathaniel Friedman—mentioned Durant only twice in the book: on the final page and later in the book's afterword. There, he described the future of Durant and the NBA with references to today's stars such as LeBron James and past players like Kevin Garnett and Tracy McGrady.

Friedman wrote that LeBron James—often pegged as the game's best player—is "terrifying in his ability, strength, and athleticism" but that Durant's talents are "harder to pin down." He continued, saying, "What makes Durant so unique is that when he's on the court, you feel like you're bearing witness to *something happening*. He's not changing the game like LeBron... and yet Durant just feels like one of the best players in the league, one who will only get better."

In the summer of 2016, Durant finally became a true champion. He led the United States men's basketball team to a gold medal in the Rio Olympics in Brazil. Durant, then twenty-seven years old, had already won gold in London in 2012. But this time basketball fans saw him differently than when he was a gangly kid drafted one year out of college.

Many still saw him as second or even third best, a far cry from the most interesting or most talented player in the league. And many more considered him a villain for leaving his longtime team in search of a championship. But no matter what you think of the kid from just outside Washington, DC, Durant's story is one of the most inspirational in sports today.

1

Tall and Long

Kevin Durant was born on September 29, 1988, in the nation's capital. Kevin grew up outside of DC, in Seat Pleasant, Maryland. Kevin and his family lived in the slums of Prince George's County, a long way over the Potomac River from the White House.

Kevin's mother, Wanda Pratt, was twenty-one when Kevin was born. His mother worked hard to raise her son, mostly as a single parent. She worked shifts at night loading postal trucks to earn enough money to make ends meet. It was a tough childhood for Kevin despite plenty of support from his mother and her family.

Durant's close relationship with his family—especially his mother, Wanda—has helped him build a long and successful career in the NBA after starting his life in poverty.

"We moved five times," Durant told *Rolling Stone* in 2016 about his childhood. "I went to seven different schools."

Despite living in the same city, Kevin's father, Wayne Pratt, was not often present in his son's early life. Pratt was a security guard in Washington, and though he sometimes helped out the family, he was not much of a father figure for Kevin when he was young. Kevin sometimes saw him in the neighborhood but had little to do with Pratt until he was older.

"I remember we were driving home one day, and I look over out the backseat, and I see him in a car with his homeboys at the light," Durant told *GQ* in 2015. "I wanted to be like, 'Ma, that's Dad, right?'"

Wanda and her mother worked together to raise Kevin and to provide him with a good home. His aunt, Pearl, was also a major influence early in his life. Although his family was very poor, Durant said he had a good childhood. He remembered listening to music by Rick James in his grandmother's house while she cleaned.

Kevin had a difficult relationship with his father, who often left his family only to later come back into his and his brothers' lives. Kevin was always excited when his father was around, but the instability of his household was difficult for him.

"He would pick me up from school. Me, him, and my brother would just chill and play video games together and go eat before we go in the house," he told *GQ*, remembering a time when his father was in his life. "Having a dad around for that year, year and a half, it was just like, Man, this is so tight! I wish we could have had this every single day."

His father did come back for good when Kevin was sixteen and his basketball career started to take off. Before that, though, Kevin had a tough time in school. He was a quiet child growing up and struggled to make friends. He grew quickly. He was tall and bony and had big feet. Kids at school called him Skeletor—a reference to a cartoon villain with a skeleton-like face. Later on, when basketball fans called him the "Slim Reaper," Durant balked at the name. It probably reminded him of kids making fun of him in school!

> **"I learned to sleep all squinched, with my legs curled up—it was like that till the NBA."**
>
> —Kevin Durant

Kevin's fast growth was great for basketball, but it impacted his life in other ways, too. He never had his own bedroom. He quickly outgrew his twin bed and never slept comfortably, even later in life when he was in college.

"I learned to sleep all squinched, with my legs curled up—it was like that till the NBA," Durant said. "One time, I'm home from college, had just scored 37 points, and I'm balled up on the couch, trying to sleep. I look around the living room and think, 'Yup, still grinding.'"

Losing Before Winning

Two major losses impacted Durant's early life. First was the loss of his aunt Pearl, who died of cancer when he was eleven years old. Kevin watched her die in her bed, coughing up blood before she passed away. Durant crawled into her bed after she died.

That same year, his first Amateur Athletic Union (AAU) coach, Charles Craig, was shot in the back after he broke up a fight. He died at age thirty-five, which is why Durant wears the number 35 on the court.

Durant's size and athletic ability made him tough to guard in high school. That height did give him some problems, though—he couldn't fit into his bed!

Coaches and players have marveled at Durant's work ethic and ability to improve his game. He rarely backed down from a challenge, always hoping the hard work would pay off with a spot in the NBA.

Kevin started playing basketball when he was about nine years old. His mother signed him up for basketball at Seat Pleasant Activity Center, and he soon fell in love with the sport. Two coaches there—Charles Craig and Taras Brown—helped teach Kevin the game. The school had sent many kids to college to play basketball and a few, like Michael Beasley, to the NBA.

Brown taught him about some legends of the basketball game, including Boston Celtics great Larry Bird. Brown showed Kevin videos of Bird, who mostly played in the 1970s and 1980s. There were lots of videos, but also lots of hard work. For training, Kevin ran up a hill behind the center at full speed to get faster. He dribbled around chairs or pylons to work on his ball handling. Even at a young age, Kevin worked for hours to practice skills that would help him play basketball at a high level. He even had painful workouts—like lying on his back and throwing a weighted ball off his forehead—for long hours, even through tears. His work ethic and skills as a player really impressed his coaches.

"I told him that first year, 'You got the gift of want-it-bad,'" Brown once said. "He wasn't just hungry, he was a *sponge*. He always wanted to know what he had done wrong, even when we won by 30."

The impact of Kevin's family and his coaches on his life growing up was a running theme throughout his life. Those who helped him become an NBA superstar remained close. Brown, who ran him through drills for hours and hours, even became his godparent when Kevin was a teenager.

2

The Shooter

Kevin Durant shined on the court wherever he played, which was a few different places during high school. His freshman and sophomore years were spent at National Christian in Fort Washington, Maryland. He played very well there, but he wanted to play for a bigger school and get more attention from colleges. Kevin spent his junior year at Oak Hill Academy, a school in Mouth of Wilson, Virginia, that is famous for its great basketball teams.

Kevin put up great numbers on a strong Oak Hill team, getting attention from a number of major college basketball programs. But it was a lonely experience playing so far from home. It was a very different place from his childhood neighborhood, too. Durant said the school was "in the middle of nowhere" and "dead center in a bunch of woods." Kevin decided he would go to a new school his senior year: Montrose Christian in Rockville, Maryland.

"I went to Oak Hill because I wanted to get that exposure and also work on my academics, but it was far away from home," Durant told ESPN in 2009. "It was tough being away from my family. I was fifteen when I got there...It wasn't that hard switching schools twice, being the new kid. I wasn't thinking like that."

The big stage that Oak Hill provided did help Kevin get used to the spotlight.

Kevin bounced between different high schools in order to gain more exposure and find better chances. He said he missed home, though, and often struggled to make friends.

"It was tough being away from my family. I was fifteen when I got there."
—Kevin Durant, of his junior year
at Oak Hill

Oak Hill games were broadcast on ESPN three times during Kevin's season. He played in tournaments across the country and worked with some of the best high school coaches while playing with other elite players.

Still, he struggled to make friends. He was so focused on basketball he had time for little else. Kevin tried playing baseball for a few games while at Oak Hill. He played first base but didn't like it. He gave up and spent more time on the court. He didn't get his driver's license, so all he did was go to school and play basketball. There was little time for fun or making friends or going to see movies.

"In high school, I couldn't do nothing but go home with my mom," Durant said. "I couldn't go out with friends, no pizza, nothing. I wasn't at all focused on partying or girls."

His senior season at Montrose Christian was very impressive. In 2006, he averaged 23.6 points and more than 10 rebounds per game, and he won All-Met Player of the Year. Kevin played in a major high school basketball event, the McDonald's All-American Game, and shined as

The McDonald's All-American Game is a chance for some of the best high school basketball players in the country to show off their skills. Durant shared co-MVP awards honors with Chase Budinger in 2006.

well. He was the game's MVP and made many in college basketball excited for what he could do as a freshman.

In 2006, his graduation year, many considered him to be the second-best high school basketball prospect in the nation. The top pick, Greg Oden, would become a familiar character in Durant's story. The two were often compared to one another, and their successes in high school and college were mentioned alongside each other at every turn.

Despite all the praise, jumping straight to the NBA after high school wasn't an option. In 2005, the NBA changed its rules to ban high school athletes from entering the NBA draft. Despite many people thinking Kevin could get drafted and play in the pros right away, both he and Greg Oden were forced to play college basketball for at least one season. Oden chose Ohio State University.

Over the summer between his junior and senior years of high school, Kevin made his choice as well. He got many offers from top Division I colleges, and a friend—Tywon Lawson—wanted Kevin to play with him at the University of North Carolina (UNC). Kevin, however, chose the University of Texas. Though UNC may have been a more proven basketball program and many legends, including Michael Jordan, had played for the Tar Heels, Kevin felt Texas was the best fit for him. A Longhorns assistant coach, Russell Springman, was a Maryland native and had been in contact with Kevin since his freshman year of high school.

Kevin grew even taller in high school and college. By the time he was drafted, he was six feet nine and 225 pounds. He was tall and skinny but, perhaps more importantly, he was long. His wingspan—the length of his arms spread out from fingertip to fingertip—is seven foot one. That length helps him defend and steal the ball from other players. It also lets him shoot over players that might be taller than him.

Durant's size has always made him stand out on the court. Later in his NBA career, Durant admitted he has underreported his height. He's actually seven feet tall!

Wayne Pratt

Durant's father, Wayne Pratt, played basketball in high school at Potomac High School in Maryland. He was twenty-three when he left Kevin's family for the first time. Kevin was one year old. Kevin—who took his grandfather's last name—had a difficult time dealing with his father's absence when he was young. Pratt told the *Undefeated* in 2016 that it took about a decade for Kevin and his older brother, Tony, to trust him again. Today, though, they are very close. Pratt even helped his son figure out where he would play when he hit free agency in 2016.

Though many called Durant "KD" or maybe the "Durantula" because of his long arms and legs, his father had a unique nickname for his son. Wayne Pratt called him "Green Room," which is a reference to the room where basketball prospects wait to hear their names called at the draft.

"When he was playing his junior year I used to yell, 'Green Room!'" Pratt told the *Undefeated* in 2016. "He used to say, 'Dad, you have to stop saying that.' I saw that he was going to be special. I saw that in between his 10th and 11th-grade year. I said, 'This kid is going to be a lottery pick.' I kind of saw that his game was unique for his size."

His father would ultimately be right. But college would have to come first.

Off the court, people mostly left Durant alone. He didn't make many friends, but for the most part he wasn't harassed by people in gangs and his family stayed out of trouble. There were still traumatic moments in his childhood. He once saw a neighbor get shot. A pit bull bit him on his way to the gym one day, and he learned to run down the middle of the street to stay out of trouble.

"The hood is a trap," Durant said to *Rolling Stone* about his childhood. "You're born there and die there, with nothing in between but that."

Sometimes Durant would take the Metro and ride it to the suburbs, away from all the drama of his home. Durant said it was "tranquil and cool there" and he could play pickup basketball without people trash-talking him as much. Durant said much of his focus on basketball was because it gave him a chance to make money to get his family out of his childhood neighborhood.

His family saw basketball in a similar way. His mother worked hard to pay for basketball camps and shoes so he could keep playing. Taras Brown worked for years with Durant, helping him pay for basketball road trips and keep him fed. As he grew into a six-foot-seven-inch shooter, everyone thought that Durant could become something special. And he kept proving them right on the court.

3

Texas to Oklahoma

Kevin Durant attended the University of Texas for only one year. In that one year, he became known as the best college basketball player in the country. Durant appeared on the cover of *Sports Illustrated* on February 19, 2007, and was featured prominently in a story by Grant Wahl called "Year of the Freshman."

Wahl wrote, "He's just a baby, all arms and legs as thin as capellini. Kevin Durant only turned eighteen in September, but with his soft, open face he could pass for fifteen."

Durant led the Big 12 in scoring and was fourth in the nation at 25.8 points per game. He averaged 11.1 rebounds per

Durant's explosive season at Texas marked a shift in college basketball, which often saw players develop their talents over their four years of schooling. As a freshman, it was clear Durant was the best player in the nation.

game and 1.9 blocks. In the *Sports Illustrated* piece, Texas head coach Rick Barnes said there was no question Durant was the best player in the NCAA, despite his age.

"I've had so many people tell me he's the best player in college basketball," Barnes said. "People have a hard time saying that because he's a freshman, but class has nothing to do with it."

Durant was named the National Player of the Year by the Associated Press, NABC, USBWA, CBS, and the *Sporting News*. Most notably, Durant won three major national awards for the nation's best player as a freshman—the Adolph Rupp Trophy, the Naismith Award, and the Wooden Award. Durant was the first-ever freshman to win each of those trophies.

He was named a consensus First Team All-American, the third freshman in NCAA history to receive that honor. His season scoring numbers were nothing short of staggering. Durant scored more than 20 points thirty times. Four separate times he scored 37 points in a game. He set the single-season school record for rebounds in a season (390), which was third all-time for a freshman in NCAA history.

Texas went 25–10 with Durant that season, finishing third in the Big 12. In the team's first NCAA tournament matchup, Durant had 27 points and 8 rebounds in a 79–67 win over New Mexico State. In another round, however, Texas lost to the University of Southern California. Durant had 30 points and 9 rebounds in the 87–68 loss that ended his college career. Shortly after the game, Durant declared that he would enter the NBA draft. It was time to go pro.

The Portland Trail Blazers were the worst team in the NBA in 2007. They had won just twenty-one games in the 2006–07 season. After the season, Portland won the NBA draft lottery that spring and the right for first choice of player available in the draft. Many draft experts agreed that the first pick should either be Ohio State forward Greg Oden or Durant.

Coach Barnes and Durant take a moment on the sidelines. Durant played just one season at Texas; he was one of the first "one-and-done" players who played college ball for just one year after the NBA's draft eligibility rules changed.

The Seattle SuperSonics had the second pick, and they would likely take whichever player Portland did not take. The debate over which player the Trail Blazers should take dominated the NBA that off-season. Portland even set up a website to help fans as they explained their decision process. Though Durant won many awards and dazzled basketball fans at Texas, many still thought Oden was the top pick in the draft.

Although Durant put up numbers at Texas, the team did not go very far in the NCAA tournament. Durant was seen as a pure shooter who had lots of potential but was not guaranteed to become an NBA superstar. Analysts felt Durant could grow to become one of the game's best if he further developed his game. Still, it felt like Durant and Oden were both destined for stardom. Despite all the hype, though, Durant said he wasn't sure he could play in the NBA until the very end.

"I didn't know I'd be in the NBA until I got drafted," Durant told ESPN in 2009. "You know, until it's set in stone, it hasn't happened. That's the way I think. I never said to myself, 'I'm going to college for one year, and then I'm going to the NBA.' I wasn't about to rush in to it or tell myself unrealistic things."

On June 28, 2007, the Portland Trail Blazers selected forward Greg Oden with the first overall pick in the NBA draft.

Durant went second to the Seattle SuperSonics. Durant and Oden were the first freshmen picked with the top two picks in the history of the draft. Fans at a draft-watching party at the Rose Garden in Portland stormed the floor. They believed their team made the right pick and were excited about the future.

> **"I didn't know I'd be in the NBA until I got drafted. You know, until it's set in stone, it hasn't happened."**
>
> —Kevin Durant

Sadly, Oden's NBA career never took off. Injuries and health troubles plagued him throughout his brief NBA career. Oden officially retired in 2016.

Bennett and the Sonics

The move from Seattle to Oklahoma City was years in the making. In 2006, a group led by Oklahoma businessmen Clay Bennett bought the Sonics for $350 million. Bennett threatened to move the Sonics if Seattle did not build a new arena for the team. Though Bennett and other owners claimed they wanted the team to stay in Seattle, privately they were actively working to move to Oklahoma City. City and state officials refused to give millions in public funds to help build a new arena in Seattle, and so in 2008 the team was relocated.

Durant signed a rookie deal with the Sonics that made him about $4 million a year for four years. Shortly before he was drafted, however, Durant signed a seven-year endorsement deal with Nike for $60 million. Reports later came out that another shoe company, Adidas, offered Durant more money but that he liked Nike better. Either way, Durant was a millionaire many times over before he ever played an NBA game. Now it was time to show the world what he could do.

Kevin Durant came to the Sonics when the team had an uncertain future. The players struggled on the court, and star player Ray Allen was traded to Boston before the 2007 season. Off the court, fans and city leaders tried to keep the team in Seattle as Sonics ownership actively tried to move the

Durant joined the SuperSonics just as new team ownership actively looked to move the team. Despite the many distractions surrounding the franchise, Durant was named the NBA's Rookie of the Year.

team to Oklahoma City. Despite all that, Kevin Durant shined in his first season in the NBA.

Durant averaged 20.3 points per game as a rookie. The Sonics went 20–62, losing 11 more games than they did without Durant the previous season. But hopes were high that the team was starting to turn things around. Durant capped off his rookie season with a 42-point, 13-rebound performance against the Golden State Warriors. The impressive stat line punctuated a year in which Durant made the NBA's All-Rookie First Team and earned Rookie of the Year honors. Durant also played in the NBA Rising Stars game during All-Star Weekend in New Orleans. He led the Rookies team with 23 points in a 136–109 loss. Although putting up impressive numbers in losing efforts became a common occurrence in his first season as a pro, the wins were coming for Kevin Durant.

4

Thunder and Lightning

Clay Bennett officially moved the SuperSonics to Oklahoma City on April 18, 2008, when NBA owners approved the move. The team was soon renamed the Oklahoma City Thunder. Durant and the Thunder, however, looked and played much like the Sonics did in Seattle. Oklahoma City went 23–59 in the 2008–09 season, winning just three more games than they did in Durant's rookie season.

The sophomore shooter did improve statistically, however, averaging 25.3 points, 6.5 rebounds, and 2.8 assists per game on the year. Durant again played in the Rising Stars Game during All-Star Weekend. This time, he scored a game-record 46 points for the sophomore squad and took home the game's Most Valuable Player Award in a 122–116 win over the

Durant continued to improve as the SuperSonics moved to Oklahoma City and became the Thunder. Seattle basketball fans were crushed to watch their team leave town, especially because of Durant's bright future.

Rookies team. Others around the league took notice of Durant's improvements—he finished third in Most Improved Player Award voting in 2009.

Durant's third NBA season was a statistical leap for both Durant as a player and the Thunder as a team. Durant won the NBA's scoring title, averaging 30.1 points per game. Oklahoma City went 50–32 that season, a 27-win improvement over the previous season. Durant made his first NBA All-Star Game in the 2009–10 season. He also finished second in league MVP voting behind Cleveland's LeBron James, who had many more first place votes despite having similar numbers to Durant.

The Thunder made the play-offs for the first time since moving to Oklahoma City as the No. 6 seed in the Western Conference. They drew the Los Angeles Lakers in the first round, losing in six games. Durant, however, proved impressive, scoring 24 points in his play-off debut. In the summer of 2010, Durant reached a contract extension with the Thunder, a deal worth about $86 million over five years. The contract took effect for the 2011–12 season, setting up a potential free agency period for Durant in 2016.

One of the many reasons for Oklahoma City's rise in the Western Conference was the growth of two of Durant's team-mates: guards James Harden and Russell Westbrook. As the two began to see their careers rise, the Thunder became more competitive against some of the NBA's best teams. Durant and the Thunder went to the Western Conference Finals in the 2010–11 season. Though they lost to the eventual champion Dallas Mavericks in five games, Durant had a stellar year. He led the league in scoring a second straight season, averaging 27.7 points and 6.8 rebounds per game and finishing fifth in NBA MVP voting.

Durant led a young core of talent in Oklahoma City that included James Harden (*right*) and Russell Westbrook (*center*). The trio played well together, and Westbrook and Durant became close friends during their time with the Thunder.

The 2011–12 season saw similar stats from Durant, as well as similar results. Durant played all 68 games in the lockout-shortened season. For the third year in a row he led the league in scoring, averaging 28 points while leading the Thunder to its first NBA Finals. Durant also played in his third straight All-Star Game, scoring 36 points and

Durant has shown off his individual talents in NBA All-Star Games. He won the game's MVP Award in 2012.

winning the game's MVP Award in the 152–149 West win.

In the finals, Oklahoma City upset the Eastern Conference champion Miami Heat in Game 1, with Durant and Russell Westbrook combining for 63 points. Miami's Big Three of LeBron James, Dwyane Wade, and Chris Bosh, however, were too much for the Thunder to overcome. Miami won the series in five games to give James his first championship.

Despite the loss, Thunder fans had high hopes for the future with Durant, Westbrook, and Harden on the roster. Those hopes took a hit in October 2012 when Harden—the previous season's Sixth Man of the Year—was traded to the Houston Rockets. Oklahoma City couldn't agree to a contract with Harden.

Going for Gold

Though he was originally cut from the Team USA roster in 2007, Durant later played a big role on the United States men's basketball team. He first joined Team USA in 2010 to play in the FIBA World Championships in Turkey. Durant led Team USA to its first FIBA World Championship title since 1994, winning tournament MVP honors in the process. In 2012, Durant won an Olympic gold medal in London with Team USA. Durant returned to the squad for the 2016 Rio Olympics, leading the Americans to their third straight gold medal.

Losing Harden had an immediate impact on the Thunder, who regressed in the 2012–13 season. Oklahoma City beat Harden's Rockets in the first round of the NBA play-offs but lost to the Memphis Grizzlies in the Western Conference semifinals in five games. Oklahoma City's play-off performance was disappointing, but Durant continued to shine. He improved his points-per-game average to 28.1 and added 7.9 rebounds. Durant finished second in MVP voting behind LeBron James, who won the award a second straight season.

Kevin Durant became the best player in the NBA during the 2013–14 season. He dominated the league, scoring 32 points per game and winning his first-ever NBA MVP Award. Durant's acceptance speech for the award became

Durant has shined for Team USA in international competition, winning consecutive Olympic gold medals. Here, he dunks against Serbia during the 2016 gold medal game in Rio.

famous. In more than twenty minutes, he thanked everyone in the Thunder organization. He thanked his teammates, singled out Russell Westbrook, and mentioned the fans, his coach, his grandmother, and—most importantly—his mom. Fighting back tears, he directly addressed his mom in the crowd.

> And last, my mom. I don't think you know what you did. You had my brother when you were eighteen years old. Three years later, I came out. The odds were stacked against us. Single parent with two boys by the time you were twenty-one years old. Everybody told us we weren't supposed to be here. We moved

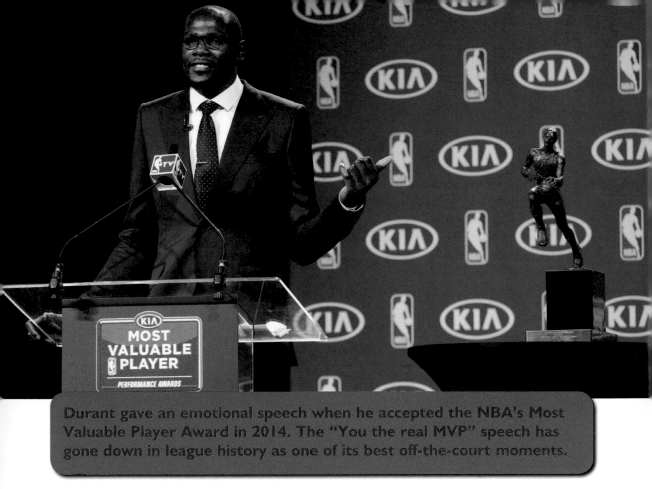

Durant gave an emotional speech when he accepted the NBA's Most Valuable Player Award in 2014. The "You the real MVP" speech has gone down in league history as one of its best off-the-court moments.

from apartment to apartment by ourselves. One of the best memories I have is when we moved into our first apartment. No bed, no furniture. And we just all sat in the living room and just hugged each other. Because that's when we thought we made it.

When something good happens to you, I don't know about you guys, but I tend to look back to what brought me here. And you'd wake me up in the middle of the night in the summer times, making me run up a hill, making me do push-ups. Screaming at me from the sideline at my games at eight or nine years old. We wasn't supposed to be here. You made us believe. You kept us off the street. Put clothes on our backs, food on the table. When you didn't eat, you made sure we ate. You went to sleep hungry. You sacrificed for us. You the real MVP.

Durant stepped back from the podium and clapped along with the crowd, who gave his mother a standing ovation. The "You the real MVP" speech was not prewritten. Durant had a piece of paper with him that day that said two things on it: "Mom. Teammates."

> **"You made us believe. You kept us off the street. Put clothes on our backs, food on the table. When you didn't eat, you made sure we ate. You went to sleep hungry. You sacrificed for us. You the real MVP."**
> —Kevin Durant, addressing his mom

Once again, however, Oklahoma City fell short in the postseason. The Thunder reached the Western Conference Finals for the third time in four years. This time they met the San Antonio Spurs, who beat Oklahoma City in six games and went on to win the NBA title. Kevin Durant was at the top of his game. But he was still searching for his first championship with Oklahoma City.

5

Quest for a Title

Kevin Durant was seriously injured for the first time in his basketball career in 2014. He missed the first seventeen games with a fractured bone in his right foot. Durant played his first game of the year on December 2, but two weeks later he injured his ankle and later suffered more injuries. Durant played just twenty-seven games in the 2014–15 season, averaging 25.4 points, 6.6 rebounds, and 4.1 assists. With Durant struggling, Russell Westbrook became a star in his own right, leading the NBA in scoring with 28.1 points per game. For the first time since 2008, however, the Thunder missed the play-offs.

Durant bounced back in a big way during the 2015–16 season. He played 72 games, averaging 28.2 points per game, and teamed up with Westbrook to make the Thunder a force in the Western Conference. While Steph Curry and the Golden State Warriors won an NBA-record 73 games, the Thunder went 55–27 and knocked off a 67-win San Antonio Spurs team in the Western Conference semifinals to meet the Warriors in the Western Conference Finals.

Oklahoma City led Steph Curry and the Golden State Warriors 3–1 in the Western Conference Finals in 2016, but they saw their lead and the series slip away in a series of close games.

Durant and the Thunder led the series 3–1 and looked to upset the best team in the league, but Golden State ripped off three straight wins to take the series and leave Oklahoma City short of the NBA Finals once again. Golden State would blow its own 3–1 lead in the NBA Finals and lose to LeBron James and the Cleveland Cavaliers.

No Mrs. Durant

Off the court, Durant's personal life is quiet. Durant dated WNBA player Monica Wright and was briefly engaged to her before breaking off the relationship.

"I had a fiancée, but...I really didn't know how to, like, love her, you know what I'm saying? We just went our separate ways," Durant told *GQ* in 2016. "I was like...We're engaged right now? We're about to get married? So I was just like, cool! I love this girl. But I didn't love her the right way."

Many people call Durant the nicest person in the NBA. In fact, companies have used that nice-guy persona to sell shoes. But it's true. Durant does a lot of work in the community to give back to others. People in the Thunder organization still tell stories about the superstar's kindness. One TV cameraman even says Durant helped him when he fell in the Thunder arena and broke a finger after a game.

"Nice isn't the right word," Royce Young wrote for CBS Sports in 2014. "Kevin Durant is kind, he's genuine, he's *just a good human being.*"

In 2013, Durant donated $1 million to the Red Cross tornado and disaster relief fund for the victims of a massive tornado that hit the Oklahoma City region. He also established the Kevin

Durant has taken time to give back to the communities he's called home, starting charities that have helped at-risk youth in both Oklahoma and the Washington, DC, area.

Durant Charity Foundation, which works with Nike and other companies to help at-risk children learn to play basketball and find positive role models in their lives.

Frustrated with his own futile championship hunt in Oklahoma City, Durant entered free agency looking for the best opportunity to win it all. There were many different ways Durant could sign with the Thunder or another team such as the New York Knicks or Chicago Bulls. Durant said the move was the hardest decision he's had to make in his career. Stay with the team he's played for his entire pro career or try to win somewhere else? He asked his parents for advice and had many sleepless nights before making his decision.

On July 4, 2016, Durant announced he would sign with the Golden State Warriors. The league's biggest free agent joining its best team shocked many fans and media throughout the NBA. Oklahoma City fans were devastated. Basketball fans in Oakland were thrilled. The rest of the league feared that one of the best teams ever somehow got better.

Durant's departure from Oklahoma City changed the way many people felt about the NBA's "nicest" player. Some thought he was a traitor for joining the rival Warriors. Others thought he was chasing a championship by picking the league's best team. Many wondered what happened to the suddenly cooled friendship between Durant and Russell Westbrook; Durant said he told his teammate he would sign with Golden State through a text message.

On October 25, 2016, Kevin Durant played his first game with the Golden State Warriors. He scored 27 points in a loss to the Spurs. The biggest moment of his first season with the Warriors came a week later when the Warriors hosted Oklahoma City—Durant's now-former team.

Russell Westbrook wore a photographer's outfit walking into the arena before the game. Many thought he was making fun of his former teammate and possibly former friend—one of Durant's favorite hobbies is photography (the NBA star was even credentialed as a photographer for media company the Players Tribune for Super Bowl 50 in 2016). It would be Durant, however, who had the last laugh, scoring a game-high 39 points in the 122–96 blowout win.

Durant's two-year deal with Golden State came with a player option, meaning Durant could opt out and reenter free agency after the 2016–17 season. It's clear now that Durant wants one thing with the remainder of his NBA career. He's won

Durant has brought his trademark dunks and athletic ability to a Warriors team that won an NBA title in 2015 and won a league-record 73 games in 2016.

MVP Awards and found Olympic glory. All that's missing is the Larry O'Brien Trophy. Durant doesn't want the world—he wants the league.

Stats, Honors, and Awards

CAREER STATS							
Year	TEAM	Games Played	Field Goal Percentage	Rebounds Per Game	Assists Per Game	Steals Per Game	Points Per Game
2007–08	Seattle SuperSonics	80	0.430	4.4	2.4	1.0	20.3
2008–09	Oklahoma City Thunder	74	0.476	6.5	2.8	1.3	25.3
2009–10	Oklahoma City Thunder	82	0.476	7.6	2.8	1.4	**30.1**
2010–11	Oklahoma City Thunder	78	0.462	6.8	2.7	1.1	**27.7**
2011–12	Oklahoma City Thunder	66	0.496	8.0	3.5	1.3	**28.0**
2012–13	Oklahoma City Thunder	81	0.510	7.9	4.6	1.4	28.1
2013–14	Oklahoma City Thunder	81	0.503	7.4	5.5	1.3	**32.0**
2014–15	Oklahoma City Thunder	27	0.510	6.6	4.1	0.9	25.4
2015–16	Oklahoma City Thunder	72	0.505	8.2	5.0	1.0	28.2

Bold= led league

Honors and Awards

McDonald's All-American Game co-MVP (2007)
Big 12 Player of the Year (2008)
Big 12 Tournament MVP (2008)
Associated Press, NABC, USBWA, CBS, and
  Sporting News National Player of the Year (2008)
Adolph Rupp Trophy (2008)
James Naismith National Collegiate Player of the Year
  Award (2008)
Wooden Award Winner (2008)
Consensus First Team All-American (2008)
Durant's number 35 retired by University of Texas
  NBA Rookie of the Year (2008)

NBA Rookie Challenge MVP (2009)
4-time NBA scoring champion (2010–12, 2013–14)
NBA MVP (2014)
7-time NBA All-Star (2010–16)
NBA All-Star Game MVP (2012)
4-time All-NBA First Team (2010–2014)
All-NBA Second Team (2016)
1st in free throws (756, 2009–10 season)
FIBA Gold Medalist (2010)
FIBA World Championships Tournament MVP (2010)
USA Basketball Male Athlete of the Year (2010)
Olympic Gold Medalist (2012, 2016)

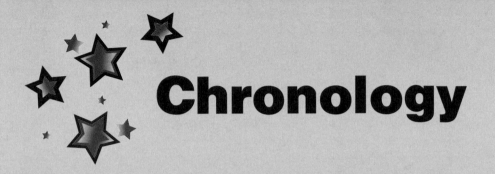

Chronology

September 29, 1988 Kevin Wayne Durant is born in Washington, DC.

2006 Durant decides to attend the University of Texas.

2007 Named co-MVP at McDonald's All-American Game, National College Player of the Year, and Big 12 Player of the Year Award at Texas.

June 2007 Taken second overall by the Seattle SuperSonics in the NBA draft.

2008 Wins NBA Rookie of the Year Award.

2009 Wins NBA Rookie Challenge MVP Award; sets game's scoring record with 46 points.

2010 Leads NBA in scoring; Thunder makes first play-off appearance.

2011 Leads league in scoring second straight year; Thunder makes Western Conference Finals appearance.

February 19, 2012 Durant records first 50-point game of his career.

2012 Durant wins NBA scoring title third straight year; Thunder makes first NBA Finals appearance.

October 2012 Oklahoma City trades James Harden to the Houston Rockets.

2013 Durant averages 28.1 points per game but fails to win fourth straight scoring title.

2014 Durant wins NBA scoring title a fourth time; wins NBA MVP Award.

2014–15 Durant suffers multiple injuries and plays just 27 games.

2015–16 Durant and Westbrook lead Thunder to Western Conference Finals; blow 3–1 lead to Warriors.

July 2016 Signs with the Golden State Warriors.

August 2016 Wins second Olympic Gold with Team USA in Rio.

November 3, 2016 Scores 39 points for Golden State in first game against the Thunder.

Glossary

All-Star Game A contest where a league's best players face off against one another.

analyst A person skilled at breaking down information.

athleticism The impressive physical qualities of an athlete, such as size, strength, and agility.

ball handling The ability of a basketball player to dribble, pass, and keep the ball away from the other team.

Division I The highest level of competition in the National Collegiate Athletic Association (NCAA).

free agency A period of time in sports where a player can sign a contract with any team.

Larry O'Brien Trophy The award given to the winner of the NBA Finals.

lockout A period of work stoppage in sports because players and team owners do not have a labor agreement.

Olympics A series of international athletic contests held every two years.

public funds Money collected from public taxes and other government funds.

pylon A post meant to stand in the way of something.

rebound To catch the ball after a missed shot in basketball.

squinched Tense or crunched up; compressed.

superstar A highly talented player at the top of his or her game and considered better than many of the league's best players.

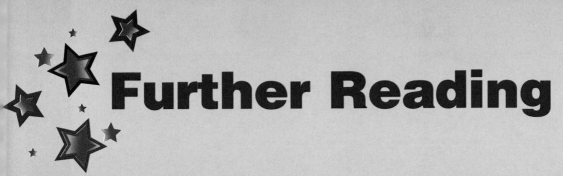

Further Reading

Books

Anderson, Jameson. *Kevin Durant*. North Mankato, MN: ABDO Publishing, 2015.

Anniss, Matt. *Kevin Durant in the Community*. New York, NY: Britannica Educational Publishing, 2014.

Bankston, John. *Kevin Durant*. Hockessin, DE: Mitchell Lane Publishers, 2014.

Indovino, Shaina Carmel. *Kevin Durant*. Broomall, PA: Mason Crest Publishers, 2015.

Websites

Basketball Reference

basketball-reference.com/players/d/duranke01.html

Learn more about Durant's stats and career.

Forbes

forbes.com/profile/kevin-durant/

Learn more about Durant's life and his endorsements.

Kevin Durant's Official Website

kevindurant.com

Visit Durant's official site to learn more about him and his charitable causes.

Index